P9-BZO-137

THE POTTY TRAIN

WRITTEN BY DAR DRAPER

ILLUSTRATED BY
SARAH DAWN ATKINSON

DEDICATED
to my daughter, Bailey Joy,
For inspiring this book with her
question to another mother,
"Did *your* boy go on the Potty Train?"
Now he really can...

THE POTTY TRAIN

COPYRIGHT© 2007 BY DAR DRAPER

ALL RIGHTS RESERVED

ISBN 0-9725396-1-1

PUBLISHED BY

WEBSTER
HOUSE

P.O. BOX 49428

CHARLOTTE, NC 28277

PRINTED IN CHINA.

Presented to:

_____

With Love,

_____

Date:

_____

All Aboard...

The time has come now, Little One,
To learn a little chant.
It will help you do do do
The things you think you can't!

If you have fear, my Little Dear,
We'll flush it down the drain!
You'll ride for sweets – a trip of treats
Aboard the potty train!

You'll have such fun before you're done
On this exciting ride!
We'll take it slow...or *fast* we'll go...
Just don't get left behind!

Now it's **your** turn to laugh and learn
A funny little rhyme,
So take your seat as I repeat
You're in for a good time...

Chugga Chugga Choo Choo
Time to make some poo poo
I'm going on the Potty Train!
Gonna be so happy
If I make some pee pee
I'm going on the Potty Train!

Mommy says I'm ready
To climb up on that potty
It's time to ride the Potty Train...
Got my whistle, got my hat
I'll sit up there till I hear "SPLAT"
I'm getting on the Potty Train!

Chugga Chugga Choo Choo
Time to make some poo poo
I'm going on the Potty Train!
Gonna be so happy
If I make some pee pee
I'm going on the Potty Train!

I'm here to stay. I'm in no rush.
I won't give up till time to flush!
I'm riding on the Potty Train!
I'll drink some water, drink some juice,
And sit right here on my caboose!
I'm *chuggin'* on the Potty Train!

Chugga Chugga Choo Choo
Time to make some poo poo
I'm going on the Potty Train!
Gonna be so happy
If I make some pee pee
I'm going on the Potty Train!

I think I can! I think I can!
Been pushing hard since I began!
I'm steaming up the Potty Train!
Although this train is very slow
I feel it now...I have to go!
I'm *movin'* on the Potty Train!

Chugga Chugga Choo Choo
Time to make some poo poo
I'm going on the Potty Train!
Gonna be so happy
If I make some pee pee
I'm going on the Potty Train!

"Tinkle-Tinkle Toot-Toot!"
Sprinkle and a poot-poot!
I DID IT on the Potty Train!
I hear my family cheer and clap...
I think I'll go for one more lap!
I'm *rumblin'* on the Potty Train!

Chugga Chugga Choo Choo
Finally made some poo poo
I engineered the Potty Train!
Time to wipe, give up my seat,
Flush and eat my yummy treat
For going on the Potty Train!

This trip is done but I'll be back
To keep my potty train on track...
ALL ABOARD for the Potty Train!

Chugga Chugga Choo Choo...
Toot-Toot!

A Note from your "Conductor"

Potty training is "a trip" indeed! As a mother of three, I personally found this part of parenting to be all-consuming and at times somewhat exasperating. BUT, I am a firm believer that one's attitude affects the outcome...So why not make the journey FUN? This is the real purpose of *The Potty Train*. There are many approaches to potty training, and just one online search will lead you to a wide variety of excellent tips and advice. This book, however, is not so much "method" but "amusement"... A simple fun "chant" if you will, to cheer your youngster on in one of life's simplest feats, yet greatest milestones...BEING POTTY TRAINED! So, relax! Climb on board with us for your next adventure in parenting! And may you embrace and enjoy each new twist and turn with your child along life's way...

Toot-toot!

Dar Draper ☺

LISTEN TO IT LIVE!

Be sure to visit www.pottytrainbook.com to download your free audio version of *The Potty Train* chant, recorded by the author, Dar Draper.

T H E